P9-CQV-724

DATE DUE

DEC 15 '07	
FEB 14 '08	
FEB 16 '08	
APR 7 '08	
APR 29 '08	
MAY 9 '08	
MAR 20 '09	
JUN 22 '10	
MAR 5 '11	

WITHDRAWN

BRODART, CO.   Cat. No. 23-221-003

just Me and
6,000 Rats

a tale of Conjunctions

To Cheri Earl and Carol Williams, who are NOT rats, but good friends. I owe you big time. And to Pearl and Yvette. Behave yourselves! And say hi to Antonio.

First Edition
11 10 09 08 07   5 4 3 2 1

Text © 2007 Rick Walton
Illustrations © 2007 Mike Gordon and Carl Gordon

All rights reserved. No part of this book may be reproduced by any means whatsoever without written permission from the publisher, except brief portions quoted for purpose of review.

Published by
Gibbs Smith, Publisher
P.O. Box 667
Layton, Utah 84041

Orders: 1.800.835.4993
www.gibbs-smith.com

Designed by Mark Wummer
Printed and bound in China

Library of Congress Cataloging-in-Publication Data

Walton, Rick.
Just me and 6,000 rats / Rick Walton ; illustrations by Mike Gordon and Carl Gordon. — 1st ed.
      p. cm.
Summary: A boy is surprised by people's reactions when he and six thousand rats visit a big city, in a tale that features conjunctions from "and" to "yet."
ISBN-13: 978-1-4236-0219-4
ISBN-10: 1-4236-0219-6
[1. Tourism—Fiction. 2. Cities and towns—Fiction. 3. Rats—Fiction. 4. English language—
      Conjunctions.] I. Gordon, Mike, ill. II. Gordon, Carl, ill. III. Title. IV. Title: Just me and six
      thousand rats.

PZ7.W1774Jus 2007

[E]—dc22

                              2007005169

Geneva Public Library
1043 G Street
Geneva, NE 68361

just Me and 6,000 Rats

a tale of Conjunctions

Rick Walton

Illustrated by

Mike Gordon and
Carl Gordon

Gibbs Smith, Publisher
TO ENRICH AND INSPIRE HUMANKIND
Salt Lake City | Charleston | Santa Fe | Santa Barbara

We were walking down the street, just me AND . . .

. . . 6,000 rats. We had come to see the big city.
We stared at the skyscrapers.
We decided to go up to the top of one.
The elevators were crowded, **BUT . . .**

. . . the people were very nice.
They let us on.

At the top I could see the entire city.
But the rats had trouble seeing through the windows UNTIL . . .

... some very nice people helped them out.

From the top, we saw a parade.
We hurried down and joined the march.
It was fun, **EVEN THOUGH** . . .

. . . we were soon the only ones in the parade.

After all that marching, we were hungry.
We had lunch at a very fine restaurant.
We ate just what we wanted, SINCE . . . .

. . . we served ourselves.

After lunch we thought it would be fun to visit a school.
We learned a lot, ALTHOUGH . . .

. . . we weren't impressed with the students' behavior.

When school was over, we went shopping.
But **NEITHER** the clothes on the rack **NOR** . . .

. . . the clothes on the salespeople fit quite right.

We heard a commotion across the street.
It was a baseball game!
We decided to go.

We had a ball, YET . . .

. . . the players didn't appreciate our trying to help.
After the game we decided to see a play.

The city is famous for its plays.

We entered the theater.

We had trouble finding just the right seats, AS . . .

. . . all the seats were already filled, **SO . . .**

. . . we sat on people's laps.
We don't know why everyone decided to leave early, THOUGH . . .

. . . it might have been that the show
was about cats.
Who wants to see a show
about cats?
We left the theater.

Then the rats saw the sign
"Museum of Fine Arts."
Rats don't read well.

They insisted we go in BECAUSE . . .

. . . they thought it said, "Museum of Fine Rats."
When we were done looking through the museum,
we went outside.

The mayor, the city council, and the police
and fire departments were there.
They were very happy to see us,
and said they would be happier *IF* . . .

. . . we left and never came back.
We had enjoyed our visit to the city.
We were disappointed that we couldn't stay.

We decided we could EITHER go home, OR . . .

GENEVA PUBLIC LIBRARY